MICHAEL C. GADWAY

JOURNEY

TO REMEMBRANCE

the Soul's Way Home

D1479325

CONTENTS

Dear Reader,

I hope you hear the waves roar-in from the deep ocean blue, and see the crowning sun bathe the mountains in orange, pink, and purple hues.

I hope you feel the crunch of leaves underfoot as you walk the cobblestones uneven and the cold wind glance across your cheek in midseason.

I hope you taste the rain falling upon your upturned lips and it quenches your thirst.

I hope you experience the harsh change of seasons: the wet spring and hot summer, the dry autumn and cold winter, as they proclaim the passing of time.

But most of all - I hope for you love. Not the love that is trill and brash, hot and cold, that flares and goes out. But the love–Divine, fathomed in spiritual and unexpected ways: the sound of God's voice heard rolling like thunder in your ears, the touch of spirit that shudders up your spine, the fragile peace and bliss found deep in meditation.

It seems to me that profane is near always loud and sacred is near always quiet. So, I ask you to keep your love for God silent, safe, and secret. Don't boast of it or take pride in it or take it for granted. Nurture it with moments of shared aloneness and whispered assurances.

I do not hope for you money, possessions, or fame, for these things only leave us wanting more.

If you experience the love of God, both human and Divine. You will find it heals and transforms, supports, and redeems.

Love is God as the person who stands with you when all others have fled.

So, I call upon love as herald to your future, though it is not my heart to give, but yours to gift each other.

Michael

THE INTRODUCTION

I dreamt a dream of seasons
That well-marked the passage of time
Till I woke to the splendor of my soul
And left even the dream of time behind

The greatest heartbreak of human existence is that we have forgotten who we are. All suffering originates from our failure to realize the truth of our being. Ignorance of our innate divinity is the source of war, racism, inequality, and injustice; it is the tragic progenitor of human sorrow. Unaware we are God light, flames eternal, dwelling in infinity, we sleepwalk through our world, darkened by our attachments and aversions, unconscious we are spiritual luminaries.

It is this forgetting of our truth that has hardened our hearts so we don't feel the sorrow of our brothers and sisters in the world. It has steeled our minds so we don't see the desperation and needs of others. It has made us deaf to their cries for help. This forgetting of our truth has made us believe we are separate from the source of all that is creation, and must therefore take care of ourselves first and foremost because no one else will.

Not realizing we are rays of the divine light; we are blind to the light divine in others. If we were to awaken to our truth and abide in our Soul-Self, we would realize that what is true for ourselves is also true for every other living being. We would know we are expressions of the one consciousness appearing as all things and all creatures. We would understand we are inextricably and eternally bound together in sacred unity.

What we do to one person, we do to all people. What happens to one of us, happens to all of us. The vibration of our every thought, every feeling, every action, and every word, resonates to the corners of creation, pushing the cosmos either towards the source or away from it. We are connected and reliant upon each other in an everlasting spiritual reality. It is not "there but for the grace of God go I," rather, it is, "there with the grace of God go us all."

If we can awaken to the realization that, at the core, we are all the same Spirit individualized, expressing in matchless radiance and beautiful diversity, different but equally divine; the boundaries that separate us will fall, crumbling back into the dust of ego from which they came. The false sense of a separate existence will dissolve into the actualization of universal oneness when we realize our own truth and the truth of all beings who share in this sacred existence we call life.

We can only interact with others at the level of awareness and consciousness we have realized. If we do not recognize and respect our own divinity, it is not possible to acknowledge and honor it in others. Most of us see God in our own graven image, but it is we who are made in God's divine image. We are drops of water in the one sacred ocean, waves on the one holy sea. We live, breathe, and exist together in a vast and connected spiritual cosmos.

The highest aspiration we can attain is one of Self-remembrance. It is a journey of spiritual awakening and its path leads to the very heart of us: the Soul-Self. To begin this journey, we must relinquish the small and contracted view of ourselves we have been clinging to for so long. We need to muster the courage to face those poisonings of the mind telling us we are unworthy and undeserving. We must accept the possibility of an unrestricted and limitless existence and all the astounding possibilities accompanying it. There is a great joy awaiting us and nothing can prevent our return to spiritual wholeness. It is the undeniable spiritual destiny of us all to become everything we ever dreamed and hoped we could be, but were afraid to believe was possible.

The journey of Soul-remembrance begins with a simple inquiry, "Who am I?" Am I this limited and fragile body, fated to grow old and die? Am I this mind, roiling with endless streams of thought? Am I my past with its joys and sorrows, loves and hates, laughter and tears, embraced in an endless dance? Am I my future with its hopes and promises yet to be, or am I something else, something more? Could I be eternal, boundless Spirit personified?

All enlightenment traditions tell us we are Souls flourishing outside the boundaries of time, space, and circumstance in this ever-present moment. We are threads of the one cloth of consciousness, uniquely expressing our blessed existence in the color of spiritual splendor. We are infinite spiritual beings using these bodies and minds to share our divinity with the world. We have only to awaken, recognize, and claim it.

There is nothing in our minds preventing us from awakening to the truth of our existence because we are not what is in our minds. It is not our attachments or aversions keeping us in bondage. It is not our fear and anger, our pride and shame, or our admiration and loathing. It is not our loves and hates. It is not the conditionings of the mind at all; it is the belief they somehow make us unworthy.

Breaking free from the puritanic cultural indoctrination that has imprisoned us in the misbelief we are unworthy sinners who must be redeemed, is essential to our spiritual evolution. It is an outdated paradigm that has become a dogmatic lie perpetuated by the organized religions of the world for too long now. We do not have to be redeemed by a God outside ourselves because we are not separate from God, and therefore not corrupt or unworthy. We do not have to plead for alms from the church because we are not beggars. We do not need an intermediary between ourselves and God because God is within us. We are eternal, spiritual beings of unlimited potential performing the role of human in a divine play. Our mistake is we have identified with the roles we are playing; we have forgotten this is just a play, a drama designed for us. The truth is, creation exists only for the benefit of the Soul. The moment the first Soul burst into individual existence, creation spiraled outward. And likewise, when the last Soul returns home to Spirit, and is no more, creation will spiral back in on itself and cease to exist.

If we can awaken to our mystic truth, we can leave behind the fallacy of spiritual, moral, and material impoverishment. Our greatest adversary is ignorance of our own spiritual stature. It is our unknowing of the truth that we must overcome. We must once again become conscious of our eternal spiritual reality and awaken to our godly nature.

We can awaken to our divinity, and with this awakening comes the gift of being able to inspire others to awaken. Sharing our uplifted consciousness is a priceless and selfless service to the world. When we realize we are rays of the one sun, the power of our spiritual light to illuminate, uplift, and enlighten, transforms all who come in contact with us. When we realize the truth, we uplift the quality of nature and its vibrations, elevating the unified whole to new levels of spiritual evolvement. We raise the consciousness of the entire cosmos when we awaken to the divinity within that is silently waiting and observing behind the mind.

We are all called to undertake only one spiritual duty during this lifetime: to wake up and remember the truth. We do not have Souls. We are Souls. We are God light, shining out for all the world to see. We are eternal, unending, glorious beings of indescribable beauty, but have simply forgotten the radiance and splendor of our being. We have forgotten the Self. It is time to journey home to that place of spiritual majesty and illumination. It is time to awaken to the truth of our being. It is time to begin the journey to Soul-Remembrance.

THE FLOW OF GRACE

It was as if I had stepped into a great ocean current,
surging within itself toward the source.
It moved without moving, flowed without flowing,
coursed without coursing
...and I lost myself in it.

There is a universal and divine intelligence abiding within us and we can learn to rely on it. It reveals to us who we are and how to navigate the world. This intelligence never falters and never misleads, it will not negotiate and cannot be bargained with. It will not enter into a discussion or argue outcomes, and cannot be reasoned with or outwitted. It does not speak kindnesses to us, placate us gently, or flatter our vanity. It is unconcerned with how we feel about it or how we perceive it. We can choose to listen to it and participate with it or we can resist it and ignore its guidance. But it speaks only truth and it gives only clarity.

It is the voice and vibration of God resounding within our very being, guiding and leading. It is heard as the small, still, quiet voice of intuition whispering to us. It is the blessed gift of the Soul-Self to know-by-knowing. The noiseless wisdom echoing across our consciousness when we are peaceful enough within to hear it, is the voice of God speaking to us. If we listen to it and abide in it, we are living in, and by, grace.

Grace is not a power external to us. It is not the actions of a capricious God who intercedes for us when we cannot do something for ourselves. Grace is the forever consciousness-presence of God within us, speaking truth and leading us towards our highest good. In this consciousness-presence, duality does not exist; there is only truth and righteousness, light, and existence. Any power contrary to the consciousness-presence of God within, dissolves into the nothingness from which it came, leaving only clarity, pureness, and perfection. The more aware of this universal intelligence within us we are, and the more we participate with it, the more influential it becomes in our lives. The flow of spirit from within relentlessly moves us in the direction of our highest good. When we step foot on the path of any enlightenment tradition, the intelligence Divine within us seemingly begins to ruthlessly conspire to bring its prodigal child home. A protective embrace enfolds us and the spirit of God indwelling awaits its opportunity to return us to the source. If we can accept this and deeply align ourselves with it, a great peace settles upon us, and the lightness of existence-being arises from within us.

To participate with this Divine intelligence is to begin to regain our destined spiritual status. To do this, we need to practice many small moments of courage. The individualized spirit of God that we are, is undisturbed and unmoved by the pressures of the world, the mores of society, and the doctrines of church. The Soul-Self communicates and expresses an unyielding authenticity that reflects the purity of spirit. It does not tell us who we should be; it reveals who we are. This gift means we do not have to rely on anyone or anything outside ourselves to guide us towards our inevitable spiritual destiny. The knowledge of our life course pours forth from within as sure as the river wanders to the sea. It needs no directive; it unerringly weaves its way home and we can flow with it. River Soul bends and curves and forks and changes directions, but it is always returning to Spirit Sea.

The less we resist the universal Spirit within us, and the more we listen and participate with it, the more influential it becomes and the quicker and surer the return home. We simply have to learn to listen better, in this moment, to the unerring knowledge of Spirit within us. But this requires an act of faith and courage because Spirit does not tell us what to do tomorrow or next month or next year; it tells us only what to do now. It will not reveal what will happen by following its lead. It asks us to trust it knows the best way home. Part of the spiritual growth process is to be Spirit led, and to be Spirit led is to live in and by grace. To live in grace is to be anchored in the timeless consciousness-presence of God within us, and listen and act in accordance with its pronouncements. As we learn to follow the directions of God within us, the separate sense of existence we call ego begins to dissolve and lose its delusive hold over us. When we live in this way, we live a consecrated life of enduring grace that expresses the perfection, beauty, and elegance of universal Spirit within.

Error and confusion have no place in this consciousness-presence because ego has no footing here. There is no me and God, or me and you; there is no separate sense of existence at all. There is only the we of God expressing as the individual consciousness you see before you, and it is moving untiringly towards the source. When we realize and acknowledge inwardly that Spirit infallibly guides us even though it may appear otherwise, we begin to accept and understand we are not the doers. The only power and the only expression of that power is God, and God as the one force and the one demonstration of life resides within us. When we are anchored in this consciousness-presence; relationships, events, and experiences appear to unfold and evolve in perfect harmony with Spirit. While it may seem as if Spirit is reaching out into the world to move and arrange events and circumstances for our benefit, in truth it is we who are now aligned with the unerring will of God within us, and synchronized to its flow. The intelligent will of God is always and unfailingly guiding us in the direction of spiritual fulfillment. The material world then appears to the outside observer to align, support, and order itself for us, when in fact, it is we who are aligned with Spirit expressing as our world. We do not have to reach out and take anything; we have only to reach in and accept everything. With this awakening comes the realization that the perfect path and direction was already laid before us, waiting for us to take it up and follow it.

As spiritual beings experiencing humanity, we are each born into this world with a unique and brilliant soul providence. There is a righteous and correct passageway through life built into our destinies by the intelligence that is Spirit. When we accept we have a spiritual purpose awaiting us, and when we take it up and willingly and consciously participate with it, life spontaneously unfolds and flows without the effort or complications caused by the ego's involvement. Though there may be challenges to overcome as we grow and expand in this consciousness-presence, and we may have to work hard, we still live a life embraced in the spirit of God.

We don't have to force life to unfold or make things happen. Knowing that Spirit only moves in the direction of our highest good makes manipulating our world in the forges of our imagination, or trying to create our environment using the mind an act of egoism. This stems from the mistaken and poor rationalization that claims we are the co-creators. But to do so only ensnares us in the complications of ego and the delusion of the material world further. We do not need to conjure perfect circumstances into our lives; they are already there waiting for us to recognize and accept them. The grace and power of Spirit within has already done the work for us; we simply have to surrender and accept its blessings. Realizing this, we know we do nothing, Spirit within us does the work. We have learned the river of life flows all on ts own and we do not need to paddle with or against the current.

When we attune ourselves to the consciousness-presence of the Divinity within us and anchor ourselves in it, we are abiding in grace. We then move and breathe in harmony with the intelligent will of God, and that will is for us to experience perfect fulfillment. The intelligent will of God is to thrive and flourish and to be successful in all ways as we move towards the realization of truth, towards the source. Our experiences in the world are then a direct reflection of the consciousness Divine within. When we are abiding in grace, that consciousness-presence within, our choices and actions are a reflection of Spirit's perfection as are the results.

But the choice to abide in the perfection and power of grace is ours. We can either listen and participate with the consciousness-presence within us and follow its unerring directives, or we can ignore its guidance and continue struggling through life, living in ignorance of our own divinity. When we become aware of the consciousness-presence silently waiting within to guide us, a simplicity of choice presents itself; "Will I listen and follow the guidance of the spirit of God within me or will I, the ego, ignore and break away from grace and go my own way?"

THE CLOUDS

Its simple beauty boast of such renown
the clouds fell the mountain down.
But still a darkness came to me, not as loss of light or sun
but by the hopeless thoughts I'd spun.

W e are luminous beings of sacred, Spirit-light called Souls, immortals with the capacity for unparalleled greatness. If we are, at the core, beings of pure and unadulterated Spirit, why is it we remain unaware of this truth? What is keeping us from experiencing our divinity? Why are we not already awakened to the spirit of God within us, and what prevents us from realizing ourselves as the brilliant creatures of spiritual perfection we are?

Built into our destined right and true way is the possibility of physical, emotional, and spiritual fulfillment; we can become all we dreamed we could be but were afraid to believe was possible, if we are willing to make the choice to confront and dispel the clouds in our minds obstructing our radiance and leading to us to doubt our truth. We are spiritual suns whose nature is to shine unhindered unto creation, but our mental clouds block our soul-light, preventing it from shining forth. We have come to believe we are the clouds, when in fact we are individualized and eternal spiritual light of elysian wonder. On a cloudy day, do we stand under the sky and affirm that the sun is still there? Do we doubt the sun is there just because the clouds are in the way? We know the sun is there. We don't have to call aloud to the sun to make it shine; it will shine once the clouds have gone. We do not have to claim into view, or even believe that which we already are; we simply have to remove the clouds that block the radiance of our Soul-light. When the clouds are dispelled, we as spiritual suns will shine forth in unobstructed brilliance.

The truth is, we are already that which we most desire; we are whole and complete, living in the ever-renewing joy of God. We are spiritual immortals who exist in a unified and timeless reality. We just can't see this truth through the clouds and haze of our minds. We, as Souls, interact with this world through a limited field of organized energy we call the mind. It is the mind that gives form to Spirit. The mind is a medium of communication: an information exchange and an avenue of expression. The mind allows the Soul to take in, experience, and process the world making it possible to have a relationship with the manifest realms. It is also the mirror in which the Soul views its own reflection.

This mirror can become clouded and darkened by our attachments, aversions, and when we cling to people, experiences, things, or this life. When this happens, we lose sight of our spiritual identity. We cannot see or witness the shining of ourselves as Souls. Our spiritual insight is diminished by these mental conditions which fog the mirror of perception. We forget who and what we are; we temporarily fall into ignorance of our true nature. We then begin to believe the contents of the mind, and the material world with its attractions to be the only reality. We become identified with our thoughts and feelings and then we are propelled by our attachments and aversions. Our subconscious habits, desires, and inclinations become powerful forces which drive us forward. It is our identification with the conditions in our minds that make us believe we cannot overcome them and we are not worthy to experience the spiritual reality of our existence. The more identified with the modifications of the mind we are, the more difficult it is to see the solution and believe we can escape their grasp.

Our world, our perception of it, and our experiences in it, are not expressions of our hopes, dreams, and wishes. The world, as we experience it, is our consciousness made evident. It is a reflection of the subtle conditionings and patterns of awareness that are the foundation of our thoughts, actions, and reactions. The projection of our habitual states of awareness and our consciousness is perceived as our experiences in the world. Our mundane interactions are expressive extensions of the subconscious patterns locked into our minds. When we resolve and dissolve these patterns by doing the inner work, only the light and perfection of God remains shining in the mind, and this light and perfection becomes our everyday experiences expressing outward as our world; we see the world from a different perspective and in a new light. We then experience this light and perfection as the harmonious unfoldment of circumstances and events, but it is not Spirit reaching out and changing anything for us through grace. We are now experiencing the perfect unfoldment that is the only true expression of Spirit waiting for us to align ourselves with it.

Further blinding us to the truth of our being is the relentless motion of the mind charged with these alternating currents of mental fluctuations comprised of our thoughts and emotions. The movements of these thought currents blur the Soul's perception of itself. The Soul cannot see itself clearly with the mind always in motion and always focused on its desires and yearnings. A quiet mind sees clearly into the truth of its existence; a still mind experiences the truth of its existence as its own. When the mind is as pure and still as the Soul, the realization of Soul-Self blossoms in the field of the individual's awareness.

If we want to claim our rightful spiritual destiny and experience the freedom that comes with knowing the truth, the way for us all is to confront and dissolve the restrictions in our minds that are keeping us in servitude. On the enlightenment path, self-actualization and Self-realization is an integrated process; one is not possible without the other. *"What a man can be, he must be..."* (Maslow, 1943). As we confront and dissolve the mental obstructions that are preventing us from an unrestricted existence, we become more and more cognizant of the spiritual truth of our own being.

We know the process of spiritual evolution has begun because we hear an unrelenting Soul-call we cannot ignore. We become divinely discontent with any restrictions in our minds or in our lives. We begin to suspect we are Spirit-immortals who should be experiencing a life of harmony and order. The process of clearing the clouds away begins when we can no longer bear to remain in our current state of awareness and endure the restricted conditions we are experiencing. The Soul-Self cries out for freedom, unable to tolerate any longer a prison of limitations. The need and drive for spiritual expression and realization becomes impossible to ignore. What we used to believe was coming with a future heaven, we now hunger to experience in the present. We come to understand we have no choice but to step upon the path leading us home to Self-realization and wholeness. We accept that Soul contentment will only come when we do the inner work of dissolving the mental restrictions, clouding our inner sight, and blurring our spiritual perception of the Soul-Self.

It is the ego that keeps us imprisoned. The ego is a false sense of a separate self and the misperception of an individualized persona; it is the mistaken belief that we are separate from the source of all creation and distinct from Spirit. Our attachments and passions, our aversions and repulsions, stem from the ego's attempt to remain in control and maintain its false sense of individualization.

When the ego perceives it needs something or someone to keep and maintain its sense of a distinct existence, it clings tightly, causing an attachment. When the ego perceives something is coming close that threatens its sense of an individualized persona and its well-being, it pushes it away causing aversion. From these two psycho-mental conditions, come all other unbalanced emotional states. Fear, anger, desire, hatred, all stem from the ego's attachments, aversions, and its clinging to people, things, and feelings in its attempt to maintain its perceived uniqueness. These are what cloud our minds and prevent us from seeing and experiencing the truth of our being. These are the subconscious drives, habits, and tendencies that impel us through life; when we are spiritually unawake, we act and react according to their mandates.

If we want to be free, our spiritual inner work is to dispel the mental clouds that block the Soul from shining. We must confront, neutralize, and dissolve these mental poisons and weaken the ego's hold on us. It is our egos with their attachments, aversions, and their clinging to this life that prevent us from realizing our divine nature as Spirit-immortals; the clouds in our minds keep us in ignorance of the spirit of God in dwelling. Although it is not possible to destroy the ego through an act of will, it is possible to wake up to our spiritual reality and simply watch it dissolve and let it fade away. The less identified with the small self we become, and the more we remove the mental restrictions clouding our awareness, the less influential the ego becomes. As we begin to see ourselves more and more clearly, we awaken to unrestricted spiritual insight and relinquish our limited human ego perspective.

For so long now, we have been told we are something other than what we really are, and we believed it. The hierarchal churches, and their representatives have misled us, telling us they have the power to redeem us. When the truth is, we and we alone hold this power for ourselves.

Each of us has the inherent God given ability of Self-redemption; we just need the willingness to start the Soul journey home. We are not losing anything when we dissolve the ego; we are not giving up or giving away ourselves. We are gaining everything and returning to the realization of our real and eternal nature as we reestablish our unity with the creator and the created.

Now is the time to take up our mantles of divinity and claim our rightful spiritual heritage. We can clear the clouds of ignorance and delusion once and for all if we believe in ourselves and take the necessary steps to be free. When we resolve the negative mental patterns that block the light of the Self, we dissolve them and diminish the ego once and for all. We are individualized divine beings of Spirit. We are Spirit temporarily personified. Our true nature is the eternal miracle of ethereal light; we just have to rise up and claim it.

THE SURRENDER

I no longer go into prayer and tell God
what I want or need him to do.
I go into prayer and ask God what he needs me to do...
and then I listen.

There comes that moment in our spiritual journey, when our awakening consciousness recognizes the impermanent nature of this world and our transient relationship with it. We come to understand there can be no enduring happiness or security with anything that is temporary. The disappointment and dissatisfaction inherent in this realization drives us to seek answers from the source. Realizing we cannot continue as we are, and knowing we must rely on a higher power for our needs to be met, we turn inward to the spirit of God, if only to seek an end to our discontent and suffering.

But before we can hear the spirit of God in dwelling, speaking clearly to us, guiding us, and offering us lasting happiness, we must quell the noises reverberating through our minds, drowning out the small, quiet voice of God within us. We cannot still the clamor of our shrill doubts, fears, and desires with sheer force of will though. The more we suppress and repress our thoughts, the stronger and louder they become. The way to silence the clamor of our minds is by accepting what is in them and what they present to us without judgment. We must accept this life, with all its joys and sorrows, all its victories and losses, and all its loves and hates, just as it is. But the greatest challenge we all face is accepting ourselves, as we are, in this moment. We must accept ourselves with all our weakness and strength, all our narrow and broad mindedness, and all our past mistakes and successes, just as we are.

Accepting ourselves seems a dangerous choice because we have been trained by church, society, and by our experiences to believe in our unworthiness and we are afraid if we accept ourselves as we are, it means we truly are unworthy; this is the great lie of our culture. At the core, we are complete and whole. We are Souls, Spirits-Divine, perfected beings made of God-stuff. But we have been indoctrinated into the misbelief we are not enough and we must have more to be more. Church tells us we need spiritual intervention because we are not sufficient to speak with God directly. Society tells us we need more money, more things, more friends, more of everything to be happy because we alone are not sufficient. But we don't need more from the world to be happy, we need only experience the truth of our being to realize the happiness within, and church and the world cannot give that to us.

Accepting ourselves, this world, and the lives we are living, is the great spiritual paradox; we must accept our flawed personalities and the imperfect world that is before us to experience the perfection of Spirit that is within us. Our journey to Soul remembrance is a journey of acceptance and nonresistance, and to step onto the path of transcendence and freedom is to pilgrimage through the valley of acceptance and nonresistance. This is the transformative secret that turns our lives into a sacred demonstration of God's perfection. Much of our journey to Soul remembrance is learning to accept ourselves, others, and our world without judgment.

To do this we must have faith: faith that our intuitive intelligence knows the way, faith that the spirit of God in dwelling will never abandon or forsake us once we turn towards it. Finally, we must have faith that despite all appearances, there is an escape from our discontent and suffering. Our hearts tell us this is true, and the first act of faith as we begin this journey, is to believe in ourselves and the inner knowing of our hearts.

We are called upon by Spirit within to make vital and conscious decisions. Will we confront and let go feelings of shame, resentment, unworthiness, and self-hatred, regardless of whether we believe we deserve to or not? Will we step forward to embrace a lasting happiness? Will we muster the courage needed to have belief and trust in the divine spirit of God within us? Will we surrender to the process of spiritual growth and unfoldment? Will we surrender to God?

God does not ask us to give up or abdicate Self-reliance. The spirit of God in dwelling asks us to trust and believe in our own divinity and to understand we are not to throw away our lives to any outside source. We are to trust the true nature of our existence-being knows the way home. The God of us, in us, will never falter or mislead us if we listen to and follow its guidance. But it is not possible to hear the Divine within, and abide in that consciousness-presence until we have muted the deafening cacophony of fear, doubt, shame, and unworthiness that demands our attentions. We cannot hear the spirit of God indwelling until we have silenced the dissonance of our attachments and aversions. To find the lasting freedom we seek, we must recognize, accept, and neutralize everything in our minds that is preventing us from experiencing liberation.

There is a reason and a purpose for our current circumstances. The form and shape of our lives is not random; our world and our experiences in it are the direct reflection of the subconscious patterns in and dominating our minds. What we are experiencing outwardly is the manifestation of the mental blue prints charged by spirit, locked into our subconscious minds and expressing into, and as our material world, our perception of it, and our experiences in it. Our lives are creative expressions of the Soul-Self, made manifest by the patterns in our minds. Spirit uses the mind to give form; thoughts of, and by themselves cannot create. They are powerless ripples until charged with Soul force. Once invested with Soul force, thought is expressed as the form our world presents. The form we are experiencing must be resolved before it can be dissolved; that is why it is in front of us. If we want Spirit to use the mind to give new form to our experiences, we must resolve the current form and the way we do this is by acknowledging, accepting, and resolving the patterns in our minds presenting themselves as the world before us. Envisioning the future is not the way to freedom; resolving the present is the way. It is our resistance to taking mental action to resolve our current circumstances that prevents forward motion. When we come to the pivotal moment when we ask ourselves, "Why am I experiencing life this way and is there anything I can do about it?" Spirit rouses from within and powerfully flows towards the answer and the freedom that comes with its discovery, moving us in the direction of fulfillment.

Most of us are desperate to live a self(ego)-directed life, but the small self is nothing more than the ego trying to force the world to reflect its wants and desires. If we try to force a future new form into existence in the forges of our minds through creative imagination before we have resolved the current one, the pattern is still there, unresolved, and will return to manifest into our lives over and over again; we will get stuck in an experiential loop of manifestation. There is a price to be paid for allowing the ego, via the mind, to manipulate the material world into a form we deem worthy of us. If we look closely at our experiences, we will see these patterns presenting themselves to us and playing themselves out; we get the same kind of boss over and over again even when we change jobs or get a promotion. We continually meet people with similar personalities who may challenge us. We get in the same financial situations time and time again. These experiences are evidence there are unresolved patterns in our subconscious minds that have been empowered by Spirit, expressing outwardly into and as our worlds.

If we want our world to be harmonious, uplifting, prosperous, and supportive, and to be a perfect demonstration of the Spirit we are, we must cleanse the mind of the restrictive patterns and beliefs that clutter and pollute it. We have to resolve the current thought patterns to dissolve them and move forward. The solution to our challenges is not found by allowing the ego to manipulate the world we are experiencing to suit our wants and desires. When we say to God, "I want," "I desire," "I need," we are affirming our awareness of separation from the source. An awareness of separation is a consciousness of lack and insufficiency, and further strengthens the ego. Any attempt to have Spirit conform to our will is an act of ego and the result will be disappointing, further ensnaring us in the delusion of this world. It is we who awaken to the Divine will if we want our lives to be reflections of the perfection of God. The answer is to remove everything that gets in the way of the light of our being from shining forth into the world, and to do this we must cultivate a consciousness of acceptance. The path to freedom is tread by acceptance and nonresistance, not egotistical mental manipulation. We do not train the mind to manipulate Spirit; we train the mind to serve Spirit. The world is the canvas, the mind the brush and paint, but Spirit is the painter.

For our world and our experiences within the world to be expressions of the Spirit Divine, full of the light and joy that brings laughter through tears, we need to surrender to the God within and do the internal psychospiritual work necessary to allow the Soul-Self to shine out and create our worlds anew with its light and inspiration. Just as our challenges are ours to accept, so too is the revelation and realization of wholeness, completeness, and joy. It is the spiritual intangibles we truly hunger for at the Soul level. If we want to experience something, we don't have to call it forth. We have to embody it in our consciousnesses; to experience true friendship, we must be a true friend. To experience true love, we must love truly. It is the same with prosperity; to be prosperous, we must embody prosperity.

The portal to freedom is surrender. The first surrender is accepting Soul-Self responsibility for our current spiritual, mental, physical, and material conditions. We accept that we must become Self-reliant and Self-responsible for our thoughts, words, actions, and lives. There is no blame to lay at our feet, but the responsibility for our own well-being and spiritual growth is ours, and we must accept it if we are to experience a future without restrictions and boundaries. If we wait for a God outside ourselves to rescue us and change the world we live in, we will stagnate in a false piety and a misguided belief system. If we allow the ego to exploit Spirit using the mind to create under the false assumption that we are the doers, we will enmesh ourselves in the delusion of the material world. The dangerous possibility we may never realize or experience our own divine nature and all the beauties and mysteries that express from it, will become our reality.

Surrender is acceptance of what is, with the understanding that change is inevitable. Change is sewn into the very fabric of nature, only Spirit lasts forever. When we accept ourselves, this life, this day, this moment; we free Spirit to forge ahead, creating a new and better tomorrow. To be free, we must learn to be Spirit led in all things, and the way to interact with the world is to turn inward and to move forward when we receive the inner sanction of God.

THE CLEARING

In the midst of life's chaos
and confusion, change and uncertainty,
I hear God's voice thunder across my consciousness:
"One day, One thought, one breath...one moment at a time."

When we commit to an enlightenment path, a quickening occurs. The dormant spiritual forces within us awaken and their movement is always in the direction of an expanding awareness. As we seek our spiritual truth and explore the subtle interior realms of consciousness within us through prayer, meditation, and contemplation of higher spiritual realities, Spirit kindles a purging and a cleansing; any and all restrictive patterns and limitations found in the subconscious mind are ferreted out. These buried restrictive mental influences, blocking the Soul-light from shining forth, are brought to the surface to be neutralized and cleared. This process is accelerated when we cultivate stillness in prayer and meditation. When we learn to sit and be still, the challenges and troubles of the mind and the negative mental patterns we were running from, catch up to us.

The emerging core issues rising to the conscious mind challenge us because the ego, that small sense of a separate self, has identified with them, becoming either attached or averse to them, making it difficult to believe we can overcome them. There is a false mental equivalency that occurs: we fear if we face our aversions and our attachments, allowing them to rise up and take precedence in the conscious mind, it must mean what we most fear is true or will become true. We assume if the thought or feeling is acknowledged then it means it must be true. When in fact, meaning is self-derived; we can choose what value we place on our thoughts and feelings. We can give them significance or see the nothingness of them. Allowing these thoughts and feelings to come to the surface does not give them more power and will not overwhelm us or drown us in a sea of emotional turmoil. Thoughts and feelings are products of the flowing currents in the mind; they are waves that rise and recede. They have no real power of their own, except what we as Souls give to them. When we believe they have power over us, they do. When we say to ourselves, "The spirit of God indwelling, is the only real power here," we take back what is ours and decide how we will move forward through life.

By consciously accepting our repressed or suppressed thoughts and emotions, and letting them come to the surface where we take the position of an observer, without judgment, we render them powerless and neutralize them. When we train ourselves to let the negative thoughts arise and coexist, and do not react to them or act from them, we take back our emotional investment which charged them and gave them authority over us. With time, these charged, negative patterns lose their vibrational strength and begin to still into neutrality within the mind. When we remain neutral, they lose their power over us. With practice, we simply acknowledge and dismiss them when they arise, not repressing or suppressing, just moving forward undisturbed.

Eventually we become nonidentified with them completely, and we are freed. We must resolve these patterns to dissolve them; acceptance, without judgment or reaction, is the most powerful tool we can use to do this. Most of our psychospiritual challenges do not require us to take action, they require us to adopt a new attitude towards them. But we must learn to be still and nonreactive and this takes practice. Like a hanging mobile, when one piece is held still, the other pieces shake and shudder for a while, but eventually, they too go still. We need to practice this technique of acceptance in order to become proficient at it. Then, the thoughts and feelings, once causing us to run in fear, no longer have command over us. The clouds that blocked the Soul-light from shining, begin to dissipate and the truth of our existence radiates from within. We, as Souls, awaken to the limitless possibilities of a spiritual reality.

Having mastered this technique, the emotional and mental energies we expended to repress and suppress the negative thoughts and feelings are freed and becomes ours to use. When we stop running and hiding, all the energy we spent to stay in control, instead becomes a font of inspiration and freedom.

No longer problem and fear focused, our viewpoint changes; we now see the world with Soul-sight. Its beauty and opportunity rise to greet us. The creative possibilities of life present themselves to our newly realized transcendent vision. We no longer accept the need to stay in the shadows. The illuminating sun we were always seeking is freed to light our world from within.

Following through with this process means we are, in essence, making friends with our enemies, and because we are not resisting, eventually we no longer see them as enemies at all. We discover we can live our lives with these thoughts and feelings as temporary residents in our minds. We learn to live beyond their reach. By doing this, they, and their influences, are neutralized and become nonissues. When we confront our mental demons in this way, we are moving in the direction of nonattachment, non-aversion, and nonidentification. This practice of self-actualization is inherent to the spiritual growth process; it is part and parcel of Soul awakening. We cannot run from our challenges or ignore them and awaken to our spiritual truth at the same time; it is our demons that prevent our Soul awakening by clouding our vision of the truth. Their dissolution and our spiritual realization are mutually dependent.

As we begin to awaken to our truth, we realize more and more the supremacy of Spirit is within us. We can choose how to think, feel, and live. We, as Souls, decide what is right for us. We do not need to be afraid of our thoughts and feelings because we are not our thoughts and feelings. We are unending beings of spiritual perfection. Liberation and spiritual freedom are our divine birthrights; we just have to claim them.

How do we know what thoughts and feelings are ours to confront and neutralize? We know what we must face by the level of resistance we experience. The stronger the fear and the more powerful the urge to flee is, the more threatened the ego and the more important the need to look at what we are running from and what is keeping us imprisoned.

When we are fully committed to this process, the subconscious restrictions and patterns begin to surface, and it can seem overwhelming. Many strong and spiritual people find themselves sinking into depression by forecasting what the future will be like based on the challenges of the present. But the truth is, by facing the mental demons and overcoming them, we are assuring a brighter, happier, and more content future. When we confront the attachments and aversions of the mind, we are resolving the past, clearing the present, and creating a better future. One of the most powerful spiritual lessons we can learn is to anchor ourselves in the spirit of God indwelling and remain in the present moment. We do not need to look back or ahead; the moment we have in Spirit is enough. If we can resolve what is arising in the conscious mind in this moment, all other moments are resolved as well.

Every enlightened teacher and sacred scripture have made the same promise to spiritual aspirants from every tradition for millennia. If we do the inner work, coming to terms with our mental demons and neutralizing them through conscious acceptance, in combination with prayer, meditation, contemplation, and living a moral and righteous life, we will free ourselves. By doing this, we assure liberation of consciousness and the indwelling light of God will illuminate our lives and make evident our paths.

THE AUTHENTIC LIFE

I haven't lived a big life or a grand life,
but I have lived an authentic life,
filled with great loves, gentle kindnesses,
and profound realizations.

To choose to be Spirit led in all things, is to move through life as an awakened participant. When we are aware enough to turn inward and connect with the higher reality behind the mind, the need to manipulate the world to get what we want or desire falls away. When we acknowledge and accept the guidance of the consciousness-presence of God within us, every need and every righteous desire is met by it.

The practices of acceptance and right living are integrated into every enlightenment tradition the world over. They are central principles, built into the spiritual path, designed to weaken and dissolve the ego's hold over us. They break down the perceived barriers between the individual Soul and universal Spirit. Learning to accept what is in front of as it is, and doing the right thing, regardless of how we feel or perceive the circumstances we are experiencing, are fundamental and indispensable foundation stones needed to build an authentic spiritual life. These practices also teach us to have faith, patience, and perseverance. They are the forges of Spirit that mold us into humble and awake Souls. God does not express divinity through arrogance, and hubris is devoid of creative Spirit.

The spirit of God only moves in the direction of wholeness and completeness, and its unerring nature is to support, uplift, and to redeem, and we can participate with it or resist it. Our only responsibility is to follow its infallible lead while living a moral and righteous life. By doing this, we exist in truth and wholeness and only truth and wholeness are expressed and experienced as our lives.

We are not separated from God, the source of all creation. We are part of it, made from it, and existing in it. The spirit of God is within us and around us. We live and breathe, and coexist in it and with it. There is no real division between universal Spirit and Spirit individualized as Souls, just as there is no real division between each individualized Soul. It is only delusion and the restriction of the mind keeping us trapped in the belief we are separated in any way.

Knowing and realizing we are integrated and inseparable parts of the one whole reality, makes it impossible to treat ourselves and others as anything but Divine. As we become more awake in our own spiritual truth, we can practice the principles of right living with deliberation and focus, further assisting ourselves to awaken. In the spiritual growth process, we learn how to care for others and ourselves from a spiritually altruistic viewpoint, and by doing this we cleanse our own psyches while assisting and serving the world and its inhabitants: participating in this way leaves no karmic footprint that we must clean up later.

The more aware we are, the more power we have to choose; we can choose to serve and uplift humanity or we can continue down the path of materialism and narcissism further ensnaring ourselves in confusion. By choosing to serve the upward flow of spiritual evolution, we are taking steps to free ourselves from the entrapment of this world and the enticing delusions it presents to us. We are also mitigating the negative thought patterns in both the conscious and subconscious mind by learning to choose righteous thinking and behaving even when doing so seems to be without reward.

There are principles and behaviors we can contemplate, practice, and become proficient in to assist ourselves in purifying our minds and awakening our consciousnesses. These principles and guidelines show us how to move through the world and treat its inhabitants. By implementing and integrating these practices and principles into our lives, our passage through this world is in alignment and harmony with the laws of nature and the metaphysical laws of Spirit. This alignment is in accord with the consciousness-presence of God within us. The adherence to these practices and principles helps us take care of ourselves and the world we live in, for our own spiritual fulfillment.

The practice of these principles and behaviors as an integrated lifestyle is designed to dissolve the boundaries of ego and self-absorption, preparing the mind for higher states of awareness and supporting the clear and potent expression of the consciousness-presence within us.

The process of spiritual maturity includes learning to be a caring, moral, and righteous being even though our conditions and environments may not be ideal. As we become adept at these righteous living practices, we grow and mature both spiritually and emotionally. It is part of the self-actualization/Self-realization process. If we want to have a sacred life, we have to think, speak, and act in sacred ways; we have to embodied sacredness.

AUTHENTICITY

It is not always easy or simple to navigate the material world with integrity, but as spiritual aspirants, that is exactly what we are called upon to do. The most profound way to live in this world with integrity is to be authentic. Authenticity is to exist in, come from, and express only the truth of our being. When we anchor ourselves in Spirit and abide by its directives, we are living a truthful and an authentic life.

The truth is, we are spiritual beings with unlimited potentials and infinite possibilities. We only need to wake up to this truth to free ourselves from the shackles of ignorance; when we are steadfast in this realization, we will only speak to others with kind and diplomatic truthfulness. The egocentric need to be right and proclaim our superiority becomes a hollow and insincere performance at best. When we act in accordance with the spirit of God within us, we can only come from truth and this is complete and wholly satisfying unto itself. There is no need to make ourselves larger by making others feel smaller, or place an inflated and unrealistic value on our personalities.

When we are living an authentic and truth abiding life, we lose any need of taking from others what we feel we lack for ourselves; we realize we are complete beings unto ourselves. We do not need to stand out or make ourselves seen. The need to receive ego gratification from an external locus is superficial at best. Recognition, fulfillment, and satisfaction are found in the inner realm of Spirit. Turning inward to experience and acknowledge God in dwelling as our only reality is enough.

Living in this way is living in the highest way. It is the pure authenticity of existence-being. It is genuine, not catering to the needs and whims of the personality by dressing or acting differently, claiming to be exceptional or one of a kind; the need to show the world how special or different we are is egotistical and spiritually immature. At the core we are all the same Divinity sharing its unique demonstration as us. We are universal consciousness-presence expressing as individual consciousness-presence incarnate. There is no need to claim 'different' or 'special,' we are all sacred and divine. We are all the same Spirit sharing the divine consciousness of God with the world.

To be authentic is to be and share with the world yourself, your true Soul-Self.

NON-VIOLENCE

We have a spiritual and moral responsibility to refrain from harming or intending to harm any living creature. When we remove the intent to harm from our consciousness, all hostility evaporates in our presence. When our consciousness is anchored in oneness, it is not possible to be hostile or want to harm others or ourselves. Anger and violence are not part of oneness consciousness, and are therefore left behind. The joy of existence-being found in the realization of oneness changes the vibrating frequency of every living creature in its presence.

When we have the consciousness of harmlessness and practice non-violence, no harm can befall us or those who are with us. To be conscious of the Divinity of every living being is to wish for them to thrive and flourish in all ways. There is no enmity in Spirit, there is only the universal law of love. If we are truly grounded in Spirit, it is not possible to think, act, or speak with intent to harm. We see all creatures as expressions of the same God-consciousness, and therefore sacred and deserving of our love and protection. We do not try to manipulate people like pieces on a chessboard, because we only want what is for their highest good and understand they have the right to make their own choices.

We understand our thoughts and actions have consequences and how we treat others is a reflection of our own awareness. If we truly believe in the sacredness of each Soul, how can we behave with anything other than love and kindness? The only intent residing within an awakened Soul is to cherish and protect that which deserves to be cherished and protected.

The principle of non-violence is grounded in harmlessness. It is not a passive response; it is a choice to assert peaceful thoughts and actions. Harmlessness is making the choice to think, behave, and speak with gentle kindness no matter the condition or environment, and this takes marshalling our inner resources to accomplish consistently. Often it requires practice and patience as well as moral fortitude. It is a true expression of spiritual realization, strength, and conviction.

NON-STEALING

Taking what does not belong to us reveals a spiritual and moral impoverishment and a profound consciousness of insufficiency. When we take from others what we have not earned for ourselves through work, righteous living, gifts, inheritance, or inspired thinking, we are affirming to the Divine indwelling that we do not have faith in the wholeness of Spirit as our source and provider. Stealing denies and blocks the flow of Spirit to supply and meet our needs in every way. Dishonesty and stealing turns our hearts and minds away from God by refusing the endless and always offered blessings of this life.

When we steal, we are violating the spirit of oneness and breaking the law of righteous living and like a spiritual boomerang, the expressive consciousness of lack and need rebounds back into our lives tenfold as never having enough. With this poverty consciousness comes a sense of victimization and a belief the universe and its inhabitants owe us. This belief further ensnares us in spiritual, mental, and material impoverishment, creating a cycle of poverty, insufficiency consciousness, and a false belief of oppression.

There is no lack, shortage, or scarcity in God. God is infinite potential, endless space, and unlimited supply, and we only have to realize the fount of this bounty is within us. We don't have to reach out and take from others without their permission, we need only open to the infinite potential within us and accept its Godsends. Doing this does not mean what we want will magically drop into our laps, but possibilities will present themselves to us and allow us the opportunity to make our way to prosperity and abundance, often through hard work, self-improvement, and the unfoldment of supportive circumstances while our needs are met without conflict or discord.

There is a simple and certain path to abundance and prosperity that works without fail; if we want God to take care of us, all we need to do is take care of God's people. If we want to effortlessly be taken care of by the unbounded spirit of God within us, we need only serve others. When we selflessly serve others and the evolutionary forces of Spirit, we open ourselves and our lives to the abundant and endless supply of the spirit of God and all it provides. We acknowledge the oneness of spirit when we integrate selfless service to others into an authentic, honest, and righteous life.

CONSERVATION OF VITAL ENERGY

We cannot be all things to all people; we must learn to rightly use our energies. Our spiritual, emotional, and physical vitality must be directed and managed with wisdom, patience, and planning. In order to have the fortitude to pursue spiritual liberation and make our way home to the oneness of Spirit, we need to conserve and carefully control and direct the life force that flows through our bodies and minds.

If we waste our energy on useless or frivolous activities and thinking, such as over socializing or indulging in sensual pursuits that are without an even exchange of energy and emotional gratification, we will not have the strength to navigate this world with the conscious intent needed to free ourselves from its delusive grasp.

There should be an even exchange of energy when we interact with the world at large. If there is a negative polarity and our energy is always being directed or drawn outward, we will eventually lose our spiritual strength and focus.

Soul force, the energy the Soul uses to enliven and animate the body and brain, enters through the medulla oblongata. It is then distributed throughout the system to keep us alive. This Soul force is an intelligent and quantumly entangled energy that will always move in the direction of higher awareness if allowed.

When we waste this energy by permitting or encouraging it to excessively flow out into the world, we risk the possibility of not having sufficient amounts to stabilize cellular intelligence and efficiently manage our physical and mental systems. This in turns places our health and wellness in jeopardy.

Mindful conservation of our vital Soul force becomes a priority when we are committed to a Soul-Self awakening path. We cannot afford to squander our energetic reserve on pseudointellectualism, gossip, vanity, and overindulgences; these things burn away our spiritual energy in empty mental and physical activities. Our minds and hearts must be focused on the goal of awakening to the truth lying silently within us. We need to choose what is more important to us: God or the material world and all its seductions.

NON-GRASPING

We are spiritual pilgrims, traveling through the world on our way to a higher consciousness-reality. Our existence is eternal but our lives are fleeting. We are moments of Divine expression, consciousness interacting with consciousness. We are here to serve, to learn, and to remember our Divinity. Life is not a journey of acquisition and accumulation; it is a journey of Soul awakening and liberation.

If we acknowledge the lasting nature of reality, we have to accept that nothing in this material world lasts, and is therefore not real. Knowing this, we understand that trying to hold onto people and things forever is not possible. When we hold too tightly, we cling and become attached. Attachment to anything or anyone becomes dependency, and dependency is incongruent with spiritual, psychological, and emotional growth; we cannot grow in spirituality and cling to the material world at the same time.

Spirituality and grasping are in direct conflict with one another. When we resist change because we are afraid we will lose our grasp, we slow our own growth and evolution towards freedom in Spirit. All things this side of pure existence-being are subject to change and have a beginning and an end. We cannot control this by holding on tightly and resisting its inevitability. Transformation, evolution, and change are inherent to the expression of nature and its laws. We cannot alter the ebb and flow of nature; it is the way of things.

As spiritual seekers, we learn to hold everything as if it were borrowed: gently, carefully, and responsibly, with the understanding that sooner or later, we will have to return it to the true owner, God. Nothing lasts forever except Spirit. To resist the flow of the ever-changing world before us is to ensnare ourselves in the wheel of existence rather than grow, learn, and set ourselves free with the realization of our true nature. On the spiritual path, we learn to accept, surrender, and release everything that is beyond our influence. We give the burden of control and direction to the consciousness-presence within us, God.

WHOLESOMENESS

The consciousness-presence within is always leading us in the direction of wholeness, purity, and upliftment. When we listen and are led by the spirit of God, we learn to make choices which are entirely beneficial for our highest Soul-good.

Wholesome choices support our spiritual unfoldment and help us to be radiant vessels through which Spirit can effortlessly express and effectively interact with the world. These choices include everything we consume spiritually, mentally, and physically.

The religious organizations we participate with cannot be only for the purpose of socializing or they will not feed the Soul, they need to be foundations upon which we can expand our awareness. Training us to connect with the spirit of God within, and supporting us in that effort should be their primary goal; a purity of message needs to be maintained by these organizations. If we belong to an organization that preaches a message of damnation and sin, we begin to believe we are unworthy sinners rather than the spiritual giants we are. When we enter the hall of any religious organization, we should feel an immediate upliftment and when we leave its hall, we should feel a sense of great peace and fulfillment. If this is not what we perceive or sense, then it is not pure and not for us. The company of saintly and holy people has a powerful influence over us; we need to be very careful and selective with whom we seek God.

he taking in and processing of information influences our ways of linking and our states of awareness. The consumption of information om outside sources can either support, uplift, and clarify our mental ates, or pollute them.

/hen we search outwardly for information, we need to be informed, ot validated. We can seek out sources that help us expand our points f view or we can watch and listen for sources that validate us in our jnorance. We have the power of choice when it comes to taking in nformation that informs and uplifts, and we should be vigilant in laking sure it is pure, clean, and wholesome. We can choose the style nd presentation of what we watch and listen to, and this choice has direct effect on our consciousnesses. We can limit the amount of egative information the media relentlessly streams at us by simply urning off the television, computer, and radio while resting in the tillness of silence. The world moves forward whether or not we are verly involved.

)ur food choices are indicators of our consciousness. When we at healthy and vibrant food, we are supporting ourselves not only hysically but emotionally, and spiritually as well. The food we choose an reveal our internal states of awareness. There is a simple way to)ecome more aware of our food choices and assist ourselves to higher tates of awareness. The awake and aware way to eat is to use the three I's. We can ask ourselves these three questions: Is it **Healthy**? Does it nake me **Happy**? **How much** is enough?

CONTENTMENT

We can train ourselves to be centered and calm under all circumstances. We can be Soul-content by turning inward and connecting with the consciousness-presence within. It is our resistance to the changing scenery and our emotional investment in it that causes us to be mentally disturbed or upset.

There is a timing and a rhythm to life and if we watch, as an awakene observer, life will unfold without us needing to manipulate or contro it. We will be amazed at the beauty and synchronicity of life's flow whe we can observe it from a place of stillness.

Contentment is not trying to be happy regardless of the circumstance we are experiencing or playing the role of a Pollyanna. Contentmen is training ourselves to be inwardly calm and equanimous knowin what is presented to us is a drama, and like all things in this world wi change and fade away.

We are not our feelings; our feelings are waves in our minds that rise an recede, and we can choose to react to them immaturely or respond t them with clarity and self-control. Part of the spiritual growth proces is learning to discern the truth of our being from the body and mind When we know what we are by experiencing and realizing our divinit we don't allow our thoughts and feelings to push us around and dictat to us. We remain centered and Soul Self-aware.

By remaining centered and Soul-awake, we can make choices rathe than decisions. Choice comes with awareness; decisions are most ofter subconscious reactions to life's delusive drama. The more awake we are and the more Soul content we become, the more choice we have.

MODERATION

Pursuit of the Divine doesn't mean we have to give up enjoying life and its benefits. But it does mean we cannot allow ourselves to become emotionally co-dependent on anyone or anything. Moderation is sleeping when we are tired, eating when we are hungry, playing when it is time to play, and working when it is time to work without self-indulgence or over exuberance, and without attachment.

We can learn to live the life that has been given to us with responsibility and gratitude and still enjoy each moment for what it has to uniquely offer. But, when the moment is over, move on to the next moment with optimism and attention. Obsession and attachment are the enemies of wisdom. If we find ourselves unable to function or move through our day without something or someone, we are not mentally and emotionally balanced and we are not practicing moderation.

If we find ourselves obsessing or dysfunctional because we cannot have something we want, we need to take action to adjust our viewpoint and lifestyle. We can train ourselves to be Self-contained and Self-fulfilled and practice equanimity during all the phases and changes of life.

We can train ourselves in moderation by choosing to accept from life the good, uplifting, and spiritual, without clinging and we can simply say no to negativity and hatred, and to people, circumstances, and experiences that deplete our resources and damage our self-esteem.

Practicing moderation in all things is a spiritual exercise that trains the body and mind to be reliant solely on the Divine. When we strengthen our willpower by learning to be Self-reliant and resist dependency, we are taking action steps to dissolve the ego and expand our Soul awareness. True spirituality is not the extremism of over indulgence or severe austerity. God is found by the equanimous mind, and practicing moderation in all things brings both calmness and composure to the restless mind.

SELF-INQUIRY

There are three questions every spiritual seeker should ask on the awakening path. What am I? What is God? What is my relationship with God? These questions form a contemplation triad that expands individual awareness and makes more transparent the border of ego. The mind may not be able to grasp the answers to these questions, but in the attempt to understand, we expand our awareness and transcend the mind, fortifying the reality of our spiritual existence.

The process of spiritual growth often begins when we question the validity of our traditional, religious, and spiritual paradigms. What do the saints and seers mean when they tell us we are immortal beings and gods of spirit and light? When we are told the kingdom of heaven is within us and God is within us, are we to take this as literal or as metaphorical?

The most powerful tool at our disposal for spiritual evolution and Soul-Self-discovery is our ability to still the mind and gently inwardly inquire into the truth of our own being. When we temporarily dismiss our observation bias of the world and pull our senses within, we allow Spirit to shift our awareness to new and higher levels of perception. We give ourselves the opportunity to realize we are not what our senses and the world have been telling us when turning inward and focus on the transcendent aspect of our being.

Self-inquiry is more than an intellectual exercise. It is a direct and unbiased probe into the reality of our existence-being. It is divine contemplation made practical. When we place any one of the contemplation triad questions on the tableau of our minds and unremittingly inquire into their meaning, Spirit is bound by our desire to answer. The answers to these questions do not come to us as thoughts, they come as revelations and realizations. The Soul's ability to know by knowing is experienced and the reality of existence is realized. Revelations and realizations are irrevocable and permanent. Once we have realized the truth, that at the core, we are immortal spirit, no one can tell us otherwise.

DEVOTION

If we want to experience the joy and bliss that come with the realization of the Soul-Self and all the uplifting and fulfilling experiences that come with it, we have no choice but to put God first. Devotion is dedicating and committing ourselves to the awakening process no matter the challenges or difficulties presented to us.

Devotion isn't the emotional drama of overly demonstrative people. It is often a quiet sense of purpose that expresses itself as the relentless inner pursuit of the Divine. When we are devoted to God or the awakening process, we keep what is sacred and valuable to us private and protected. We don't have to dramatize our love for God; it is a personal matter that should be kept sacred and close to our hearts.

Usually change in our consciousness happens slowly, over time, and it is profoundly personal and not to be shared with casual seekers. To experience these changes, we have to be patient and persistent and this requires devotion. When we are devoted to awakening, we commit ourselves by vowing to the indwelling divinity of God, and no one can dissuade or alter us from our committed course.

We strengthen our minds and bolster our hearts when remain true to our oath to never give up until we have found God. When we know our path to liberation of consciousness, we take each step with the knowledge we will never quit or acquiesce to the pressures of society and the material world; we know we will always put God first.

THE WAY HOME

I am the song I am the poem
I am the road and the long walk home

Every road home is a good and righteous road home and there are as many roads home as there are Souls to travel them. All enlightenment traditions lead to the same realization though; we are at the core spiritual beings of God light and wonder, unbound by time, space, and circumstance. No matter which tradition or spiritual path we are on, the process is the same; enlightenment and liberation come when the ego is dissolved, our false belief in a separate reality is permanently ended, and we awaken to the truth of our existence-being.

The dissolution of ego does not happen as a result of willpower. We cannot force the separate sense of existence to dissipate. It is a result of the expansion of awareness and the fullness of consciousness expressing unhindered. It may come quickly as a result of previous effort or slowly over time with patience and what seems like hard work. But we can participate joyfully with the process if we allow ourselves to be led by the spirit of God within, accept the path laid before us, and not resist the unfolding play of lights and shadows we call life.

All spiritual paths are journeys of awakening and realization. They encourage the quieting of the mind and the letting go of egoism and restrictive thoughts and behaviors. We cannot awaken to the reality of our spiritual existence and serve our egotistical wants at the same time. Recognizing the spiritual path we are on does not mean we must give up our livelihood or our life. But it does mean we bring a new and higher awareness to the life we are living. As long as we are honest, not hurting other living creatures, and living a righteously authentic life, what we do to earn a living will be acceptable in the eyes of Spirit. It is the awareness and the consciousness we carry and share with others while we work that makes the true difference. It is the inner condition and our awareness of God that we should place our worth upon, not how we earn a living or how we are perceived by others.

We each have our own spiritual road to tread and no one can walk it for us. We can, however, recognize the general path we are on and honor it with our attention and focus. If we keep the spirit of God alive within us by nurturing and respecting it with our awareness, we make sacred our journey home and bring meaning to our existence. There are four primary paths leading home to the realization of God and the liberation of the Soul-Self. We may be a combination of all of them, or strongly one. But when we identify our path, we should cherish it and embody it in consciousness. By doing this, we sanctify our lives with spiritual mindfulness and vital energies. Each path below weakens the boundaries of ego that keep our awareness and consciousness from realization of our unity with Spirit. No matter which path we find ourselves drawn to, prayer, contemplation, and meditation need to be integrated into it. Each time we turn inward in silent prayer and meditation, we light a candle of Self-realization in the cathedral of Spirit.

THE ALTRUIST

For some, the path to freedom is a life of selfless service and caring for humanity. By caring and serving without attachment to results or the need to be recognized, the sense of me and mine begins to lessen and the need for the small self to be front and center is diminished. By serving Spirit, we expand our awareness and consciousness. By learning to put others first, we develop the awareness of being part of a universal spiritual community as well as gaining insight into the value of philanthropy, and the oneness of Spirit.

When we contribute to the spiritual evolution of the planet and its inhabitants, we serve a higher purpose and we burn our attachments, hubris, and self-absorption in the fires of service and kindness. We place the needs of our spiritual brethren before our own when we learn to choose kindness over self-righteousness, and in doing so, we gain the capacity to let go of ego with its confines and imprisonments.

We don't have to reach out or leave our homes to begin to practice altruism. We can be altruistic with our own family and friends. By consciously putting others first, we break down the false sense of 'I-am-ness' that prevents us from transcending the mind and senses. This can be especially challenging when we try to break through the behavioral patterns established within our own families. Conscious living forces us to look deeply into our own psyches and weed out the restrictive thoughts and emotional patterns that do not serve us and our highest good. Altruism pushes us to mature emotionally and spiritually by learning to be strong and humble at the same time.

Living the life of altruism is not a life of servitude or subjugation. We put others first while honoring and respecting the Divinity within ourselves. We do what is best for our and their highest good, choosing to not enable or participate in any sense of dependency. We serve their spiritual needs regardless of over-dramatization and despite attachments or aversions. We do what Spirit leads us to do for their and our highest good and spiritual growth. This is not to say we must remain in abusive relationships, familial or otherwise. There are times in our lives when we may have to walk away. But we don't have to walk away out of anger or the inability to forgive. We can love and bless them as we go our own way. We know we need to walk away when staying would disrespect the Divinity within us, and violate the sanctity of the Spirit indwelling.

The path of altruism is not evidenced by apparent martyrdom. It is a quiet path filled with doing the right thing regardless of circumstances or perceptions. It is marked by kindness and generosity of spirit, not by the need to be seen. It is not the narcissistic behavior of those who have a savior complex. Altruists don't need to be recognized or put on a pedestal. They do what they do because it is the right way for them and they know it. They don't need to be praised or honored for doing the right thing, nor should any of us. The motivation of an altruist is selfless service without a need for recognition. To be altruistic is to serve Spirit in the truest sense. We give and care because it is our spiritual responsibility to do so. Living a life of selfless service reflects the consciousness of unity and integration of Spirit and Soul.

Altruists realize when we serve others, we are helping in the upliftment of humanity and the upward progression of spiritual evolution. When we serve without expectation of reward or recognition, we share the spirit of God within in the highest way. It is consciousness awakening and caring for consciousness.

THE SAGE

The path of wisdom is not the path of intellectualism, it is the way of right understanding and discrimination. Wisdom is the result of the Soul's ability to know-by-knowing. The sage is someone who can recognize truth from falsehood and act accordingly. A sage can distinguish between the real and the unreal, the lasting from the temporal, and Spirit from nature.

Recognizing truth is not a function of the mind; it is an intuitive gift of the Spirit. We know what is true and untrue not because we are told or because we learned it in a classroom, but because we as Souls inherently know what is of us and what is foreign to us.

When we listen, truly listen, to the small still voice of God within us, we hear the truth of Spirit indwelling. The truth is a unified extension of our existence-being. It is part of us and intrinsic to us. That is why some people say they "hear" the truth. Truth rings like of bell within us when we hear it, read it, or experience it. It is in harmony with the core of our being. Truth is a synchronistic alignment of Spirit and nature, and we as Souls have the capacity to recognize when truth is present.

No religious organization can ordain the title of sage. No degree from a university or college can confer the title of sage, and no governmental organization can appoint the title of sage. Wisdom does not necessarily come with age, or is restricted by youth. Often it is the wisdom of children that rings boldest because there is no mislearning to get in the way of truth recognition. They simply state, not always at appropriate times, what they know to be true.

Sages, foremost and clearly, see and hear the truth of their own being. They know what they are at the core from a known-by-knowing realization. There may or may not be any grand spiritual experiences of lights, bliss, and the sound of AUM ringing in their ears. It is not something to be broadcast or announced to the congregation. They simply and quietly know what they are and why they came. There is a clarity of Spirit about them and with this clarity comes discrimination. They are often straight forward, no nonsense kind of people. There is no pretense or false piety. They simply are what they are. They are often authentic and may have to learn diplomacy so as not to offend the tender egos of those around them.

When we practice and develop wisdom, we kindle the power of discrimination. We then burn our attachments, hubris, and self-absorption in the fires of wisdom. We know what we are and what we are not. This has a negating effect on the ego, thinning and weakening its influence as we grow in wisdom and expand our consciousness and awareness. With practice and time, sages clearly discern the truth of their existence as individualized Spirit we call Souls.

THE DEVOTEE

There are some of us who fill our days with devotion to the Divine and everything we do is dedicated to God. Our love for God is the fire of our devoutness and we keep it safely ensconced in the sanctuary of our hearts. We keep this passion silent and secret because it is sacred to us, and to proselytize it is to make it profane.

The way of devotion is not filled with emotion or exaggerated drama. It is not the overexuberance found in public displays of worship or adoration. It is not throwing oneself at the mercy of God in a crowded church or claiming to have a special relationship with a deity that no one else has. It is a quiet and long-term commitment to the awakening process of someone who deeply and unfailingly loves a personal aspect of God.

No matter how we perceive God, whether Mother, Father, Universal Spirit, God or Goddess, we should keep it private and sanctify it with our internalized attention. A personal relationship with God is the hallmark of a mystic and it transcends human understanding. It is the relationship between the Soul and Spirit and it is characterized by solemnity and reverence.

Devotees of God willingly burn their attachments, hubris, and self-absorption in the fires of their devotion, and the unadulterated purity of their motive is unconditionally accepted by the Spirit indwelling. The devotee of God surrenders the ego as an act of worship and love. As the ego dissolves, the devotee experiences a more profound relationship with the personal aspect of God that appeals most to their hearts. Eventually, the ego dissolves completely, the mind is transcended, and universal oneness is experienced and realized.

The mind cannot comprehend the infinite potential and endless existence-being of Spirit. But we can focus the mind with devotion on a personal God in order to eventually transcend it and experience the reality of our oneness with Spirit. It is possible with devotion to overcome and break free from the boundaries of the mind and realize universality. We do not need an intermediary between us and God. The clergy cannot do for us when we must do for ourselves. Devotion is the bridge that crosses over the river of delusion to the shores of Self and God realization. All we need to do is nurture our devotion with the soundless joy and gladness that is found within.

As with all relationships nurtured sacred by love, our relationship with the Divine will grow and expand with our uninterrupted awareness and constant attention. The personal relationship we build with the infinite will serve as the foundation for our inevitable salvation. Each time our intention is to surrender the results of our thoughts, words, and deeds to God, as an act of love and devotion, we weaken the boundary between ego awareness and the consciousness-presence of God within us.

THE MEDITATOR

The surest and most direct route to Self-remembrance and God-realization is the one that includes meditation, contemplation, and prayer. These are not psycho-spiritual tools meant only for renunciates who are hidden away under the eaves of their monasteries and nunneries. They are direct methods of insight and communication with the Divine indwelling and are intended by Spirit to be used by every person who desires a mystical relationship with God.

If we make time each day to connect with the consciousness-presence of God within, and listen to its directives, we will find ourselves unerringly led in all things and in all ways. To meditate is to turn inward and allow the mind to slow to stillness while we remain alert and focused on God. Meditation is not a difficult practice and it is not meant to be esoteric. Meditation is simply the uninterrupted flow of attention to a single point, object, or concept. It is the primary instrument we use to connect with the Soul-Self, the individualized spirit of God we are.

When we learn to meditate, we remove the need for an intermediary between us and God. Organizations and religious agents become obsolete when we can touch the hem of God's robe for ourselves. The power of Spirit then pours forth from within us without the necessity of a spiritual liaison. It's just us and the radiance of God shining from within.

Spiritual realizations and experiences do not come to us from an outside source as a result of our spiritual practices. They arise from within us when we have prepared ourselves by doing the inner work. They blossom from the core of our being and flower in the purified state of our awareness. The deeper we dive into the ocean of consciousness in meditation, the more subtle the experience and the more profound the realization.

Perhaps one of the greatest misconceptions about meditation, in western spiritual communities, is the mistaken belief all our challenges will melt away in the fires of our devotional meditations. In fact, as spiritual aspirants, we should be aware of how the process of purifying the mind works when meditating. When we sit quietly, fully alert and wrapped in stillness, the subconscious negative mental conditionings and patterns that have been compartmentalized, suppressed, and repressed are allowed to surface to the conscious mind to be confronted and neutralized. Once they have been neutralized, they can then be carried by the proficient meditator into superconscious states where they can be dissolved at the seed level. In higher superconscious states, spiritual forces flood the mind and rewrite or burn out the unhealthy and life-negating mental patterns we have been confronting.

Meditation does not remove the necessity of inner work; it is part of the inner work. It is often the catalyst that initiates the process of liberation that comes as a result of purifying the mind. This is why learning to remain the observer and watching without emotional investment is vital to the spiritual growth process.

Meditation quickens spiritual evolution and emotional maturity by providing direct and experiential insight into our spiritual identities. When we still the body and mind absolutely, we can experience absoluteness.

Contemplation is another essential spiritual procedure. Spiritual or mystical contemplation is not a type of thinking activity. It is a process used to gain insight into a specific metaphysical law or principle. We contemplate to gain intuitive knowledge without the possible errors inherent in mental deliberation. We are not trying to gather objective information; we are opening ourselves to subject insight. Through this process, we are able to remove the possibility of information bias and emotional validation, and see directly into the significance of a metaphysical principle or law.

In contemplation, we meditate until thoughts have quieted and are still or nearly still. We then take what we want to have a more profound insight into and place it on the tableau of our minds, and simply look at it with an expectation of discovery. When we contemplate in this way, we are not trying to figure anything out or resolve an issue using a thought process. We are using our silent focus to gain a subjective insight into the nature and purpose of a specific idea, concept, principle, or challenge.

We can also use this technique to resolve problems that seem unsolvable or stimulate creative inspiration to arise from within us. When confronted with a challenge needing to be solved, we can place the challenge itself on the tableau of the mind and look at it, waiting for insight and a possible Spirit inspired solution. Often the answer does not come during our meditative contemplation. Rather, it surfaces to the conscious mind while we are engaged in other activities later in the day, or sometime during the next several days. The solution simply presents itself to us: we know-by-knowing and experience-by-experiencing.

Divine contemplation can also be used as a tool to expand awareness and break through the boundaries of the mind. When we contemplate a concept, such as universal love, that seems to defy explanation and the mind's ability to fully grasp its meaning, we open ourselves to a more subjectively profound understanding. We do not need to contemplate those things we already understand and know. We contemplate those things we wish to understand and subjectively know.

Prayer is invoking the presence of God to experience a mystical connection with the Divine presence within us for the purpose of being heard. When we pray, we should pray as though we are talking to God, sitting in the chair next to us. We pray as if God is a living presence right here. Because the truth is, God is within us and around us and expressing as us. So, we can pray assured that God can and does hear our every word and thought.

When praying, we pray until are all prayed out; we pray until we are emptied of troubling thoughts and feelings and the only thing remaining is the quiet of our existence-being and the consciousness-presence of God. Once we have prayed to reach this still moment of peace and surrender, we stay in that awareness until we are sure we have been heard: then comes a release as our consciousness connects with Divine consciousness and there is an internal shift in knowing and a release of worry and fear. Once this moment has occurred, we can put the issue to rest, knowing our prayer has been answered. This does not mean we get what we want every time we pray in this way, but it does mean the prayer request will be resolved for our highest and best good.

THE PRACTICE OF "ONE THING"

Is not the soul that light ethereal
and the knowing of truth to set us free?
Is not the indwelling spirit God
the same found in me and thee?

There are challenges from within on the awakening path homeward that often test us to our limits, and to deny how difficult the spiritually authentic life can be to live denigrates the strength and nobility of spirit required to free ourselves. When we turn inward and confront the lies the mind tells us, facing the restrictions and poisons that prevent the light of our being from shining forth, we need specific tools that steady and clarify it, supporting us on our journey home.

Once we have brought the mental restrictions to the surface to be neutralized and overcome, it is possible to spend years struggling with them. But often, giving them time and space to work themselves out will eventually lead to their neutralization and our nonidentification with them. There are so many instances in life when facing our thoughts and feelings defies control, explanation, and logic, and the only action we can take is to learn to accept, witness, and allow.

We can move through this process with less trauma by training the mind

53

to focus on and practice a single action principle that brings calmness and steadiness with its observance. This is called the practice of "one thing" in spiritual texts, and it is designed to dissolve the ego and bring clarity and calm to the mental field. The spiritual masters of old knew first-hand the challenges we face when looking to free ourselves from the delusion of this world. They were keenly aware of the obstacles each of us must overcome to awaken to our true spiritual nature. They described five action principles to practice; these practices will bring devotees closer to their goal of Self and God realization by purifying the ego, clarifying and calming the mind, and amending past actions by serving Spirit with selfless thoughts, words, and deeds.

When working with the practice of 'one thing,' we choose a single principle exclusively, and willing commit to its practice for at least three months. We awaken each morning and consciously choose to look for opportunities throughout the day to put into practice the principle. Inevitably, challenges arise with the observance of 'one thing,' but they are always for the highest good of the Soul-Self. When we choose to embody a single action principle for a prolonged length of time; people, circumstances, and opportunities will present themselves to us in surprising ways. We may even find a number of obstacles, challenging our intention and practice, appear to rise up and meet us. If we remember, it is the ego that is being confronted, and if we treat each trial that comes as if from God, we are more likely to accept, resolve, and move through the difficulties with grace and dignity.

By practicing 'one thing,' we learn to let go of small-minded, egocentric thinking and behaving in favor of a more universal altruistic understanding. We give ourselves the opportunity to integrate into our awareness righteous and spiritually awake behaviors; we learn to think and do the right thing despite difficult people and circumstances. In doing so, we further weaken the ego's hold over us and expand the frontiers of our awareness towards a boundless consciousness. If we continue to faithfully practice one of the principles, we will eventually embody the principle; the need to practice stops when we personify the very principle we have been practicing.

COMPASSION

One of the most powerful practices used to clarify and steady the mind while purifying the ego is the observance of compassion. Realization of our unity in spirit and the inborn characteristic of consciousness to support consciousness results in acts of compassion. When the Soul, recognizing the unity and oneness of all living things in Spirit, takes action to alleviate the suffering of its brothers and sisters, it is acting compassionately. When we act with selfless goodwill for the benefit of others, we purify the ego and lessen the perceived distance between our limited personality-self and the limitless presence of God. Today we often see in the spiritual communities who preach enlightenment, an emphasis on thoughts and words. They espouse the use of affirmations and claiming one's spiritual truth. But perhaps a more powerful transformation would occur if spiritual communities would place more emphasis on compassionate action. Nothing betrays our level of awareness and our consciousness more than how we behave. It is not enough to proselytize spirituality; we must live and share it in practical ways.

Compassion is Soul inspired, empathic thoughts that lead to positive, life affirming, and uplifting behaviors to relieve the sorrow and suffering of others. Compassion is not dependent on whether or not we think someone deserves our help; it is a selfless act of universal love without judgment or expectation of reward. Acts of compassion do not have to be grand gestures or magnanimous humanitarian demonstrations; they can be simple, small, and meaningful such as a reassuring smile or a gentle hug. When we reach out with compassion, we are letting another Soul know that they are not alone and they have the support of God, through us, to face this ever-changing world.

Compassion is not just a kind act we give away and then walk away. An act of compassion is empathy and understanding potentized by the spirit of God within us and then acted upon. The spirit of God flows through us as awakened conduits to ameliorate suffering and sorrow; compassion is grace in action.

One of the most difficult challenges on the spiritual path is to extend compassion inward to ourselves. Often, when facing the challenging conditions of the mind, we begin to feel unworthy or somehow less as we recognize and accept the imperfections of our personas that must be cleared. During these moments of self-doubt and misgiving, we need to give ourselves permission to be kind to, and patient with ourselves. This isn't narcissism or self-indulgence; it is a spiritually aware understanding that, in this material world, transformation takes time, and as is most growth, often painful.

FRIENDLINESS

The practice of friendliness is more than a smile and a wave to a neighbor. Friendliness is treating everyone with whom we come in contact with the same kindness, courtesy, and respect as we do our best friend. It is learning to be a true friend to everyone, even strangers.

When we practice friendliness, we are embodying in consciousness a demeanor of goodwill and kind heartedness and we are sharing it with the world. We are abiding in a state where we are wishing well to everyone we meet and we want only what is best for their highest Soul-good.

Friendliness is not dependent on our mood or attitude, or the mood or attitude of the person with whom we are interacting. We can train ourselves to be so mentally strong, we are friendly regardless of how we feel or how others behave towards us or respond to us. By practicing friendliness, irrespective of our mood or others actions or reactions, we are choosing to think, speak, and behave with higher spiritual awareness. By doing so, we are empowering ourselves with spiritual and emotional fortitude.

Friendliness is treating others the way we want to be treated. When we are friendly, we are slow to anger and quick to forgive. We listen more than we talk. We care more and laugh easier. We give more than we take. We judge less and accept more. In essence, we share with others our authentic and true selves; we open ourselves and invite everyone we meet to experience the spirit of God indwelling. We choose kindness over self-righteousness. We do not force our opinions on others, nor do we need to be right all the time.

To do all this without expectation or fear challenges us to live a life with our guard down and our hearts open. This can test us because we have been trained to protect ourselves against being hurt by others by closing ourselves off from them. But, when we practice friendliness and choose to open our hearts to strangers, we also open our minds and consciousnesses to God.

Giving freely of ourselves, even to people we don't know, purifies the ego and clarifies the mind, making transparent the once opaque barrier between ourselves and the spirit of God waiting to receive us within. When we open our hearts unreservedly, we willingly surrender the sense of a separate existence and invite the consciousness of universal Spirit and oneness into our awareness and lives.

JOYFULNESS

True joy blossoms from within when we become aware of our connection to the source. When we are united with God and the Soul rests in the realization of its wholeness, the experience is joyous. The Soul's nature is ever renewing joy, and when we abide in that experience, it naturally pours forth from our inner resource; with practice, we can share this joy with the world.

To practice joyfulness, we first anchor ourselves in Spirit by deep and prolonged silent meditation. In the silence of our meditation, we become aware of the quiet. This quiet seems to have a quality and a texture to it and we can cultivate it with our attention. With practice, the quiet expands and deepens into stillness. Then, as we give our awareness to it, the stillness transforms into peace. As the peace becomes all encompassing, it surpasses understanding and transforms into joy.

The true practice of joyfulness is learning to carry the joy found in the stillness of meditation throughout the day and under all circumstances. Practicing joyfulness includes the sharing of the spirit of God in meditation and consciousness with others. To do this, we must learn to be still and get our personas out of the way. This requires surrender and a releasing of the ego. The spiritual realization of Self, inherent in profound meditation supports, redeems, and transforms us from struggling solitary creatures, to joyous interconnected beings. Through meditation, we discover the joy of oneness.

To practice joyfulness, we learn to be content in this moment in the stillness of our existence-being. This practice trains the mind to be calm and steady, focusing on the inner unchanging spiritual condition rather than the passing thoughts and streams of emotions. By focusing on the inborn joy of existence-being, we learn how to become better observers. This, in turn, helps us defuse the emotions that previously held us in bondage. We begin to identify with our true eternal joyous nature rather than the ever changing delusions of the mind and the alternating scenery of the world.

To practice joyfulness, we meditate until we have experienced the flow of joy from within and then we learn to carry it with us and share it with others through our awakened consciousness and uplifted attitude and mannerism. We are sharing the spirit of God when we share the fount of joy arising from within us.

GLADNESS

We are not all genetically programmed to wake up each morning and be effortlessly glad for the day ahead. For many of us, gladness is a choice we make; we choose to be happy and have an optimistic attitude despite feelings of doubt and sadness. When we marshal our inner resources and overcome our negative mental patterns, we strengthen, clarify, and calm the mind encouraging Spirit to more fully and more purely express through it.

The practice of gladness is not suppressing or repressing negative emotions. Learning to express gladness is acknowledging and accepting how we feel now and then choosing a positive lens through which we view the world and life.

Authentic gladness stems from being anchored in the consciousness-presence within us while living with abundant awareness of this moment. By doing this, we develop a confidence and a faith that all other moments will unfold for our highest good when we abide in that consciousness-presence.

Gladness is the inner Soul state of contentment blossoming into the mental field; it is the aftereffect of the experience of wholeness when the Soul rests in its awareness of Self. Gladness is the fruit of spiritual awakening.

One of the most effective ways to experience and cultivate gladness is by practicing meditation. Silent meditation connects us with spirit and supports us in cleansing the mental debris and returning our awareness to clarity. This helps us prioritize what is important in life and what is just mental chatter.

A more practical approach to experiencing gladness is the cultivation of gratitude. When we choose to nurture an attitude of gratitude, we are taking mental action steps towards a more positive life view. This intentional mental outlook has many well documented benefits both mentally and physically. But it is the spiritual benefits we are most interested in. Gratitude uplifts and connects us with the truth of our being; we are spiritual immortals and our nature is bliss. When our blissful nature is experienced, the natural after-effect is gladness.

In the stillness of the morning, just after awakening and before thoughts begin to surface in the mind, we can turn inward and connect with the source. By binding our awareness to the consciousness-presence within at the beginning of each day, we set a mental framework in place that encourages an attitude of peace, surrender, and gladness. The practice of connecting and surrendering to the Spirit within every morning for three months will have a powerfully positive impact on the psyche. This practice helps reroute neural pathways, cauterizing negative impressions that have been left in the mind from previous harmful thoughts and actions. It assists us in seeing new possibilities and shifting our thinking paradigm. By freeing space in the mind, we allow for the possibility of creative thinking, heretofore unimaginable. The more we connect to the source, the more the after-effect of gladness will be experienced and the more gratitude we will have. Meditation and gratitude yield gladness, and gladness has a positive life altering result.

EQUANIMITY

We are not robots or automatons moving through life without feelings, and enlightenment traditions do not expect us to be without emotions. But we are asked to learn to see through circumstances to Spirit operating behind what appears before us and function from a higher understanding. To practice equanimity is to learn to be even minded under all conditions and in all situations regardless of how they appear or make us feel.

Rather than attempt to control or deny our emotions, it is often more beneficial to approach equanimity as a practice of balance. There is a time and place for laughter, just as there is a time and place for tears. But even when we are experiencing emotions at their most powerful, we do not lose ourselves in them. When we practice equal mindedness, we learn to never relinquish the interior awareness of the Self due to the changing seasons and scenery before us; we remain the observer, watching the unfolding drama with interest from a spiritual vantage point.

When we train ourselves in equanimity, we are developing emotional and spiritual maturity and we are learning to put our egos, with their expectations and demands, second. We develop the understanding that we are not our thoughts and feelings and that we have a say in how our thoughts and feeling express and how they affect our emotional, physical, and spiritual well-being.

Spirit is the only eternal reality. All other things this side of pure existence-being will relinquish their temporary form, pass away, and fade from memory. By refining our ability to remain equal minded in all circumstances, we learn to take a step back and acknowledge the temporal nature of our human existence and the material world. When practicing equanimity, we hone the ability to realize we are not what is in our minds and our bodies. We are individual Spirits operating the mental and physical fields we call minds and bodies.

The prolonged practice of equanimity can be used to clarify and steady the mind while purifying the ego. We train ourselves to not be overly involved in emotional dramas and paroxysms and we grow in wisdom and understanding by remaining the observer under all conditions.

One of best ways to integrate equanimity is to focus on the breath when challenged by the alternating currents of life and emotions. We can consciously withdraw from our overinvolvement with the life scene before us and simply breathe. When we watch the breath, we are asking the mind to focus on a single act and it slows down. With this act, there comes an effortless shift into being the observer. When we are coming from a place of observation, we are practicing equanimity.

Equanimity assists us in making better decisions and responding more maturely rather than merely reacting to life and its challenges. This in turn empowers us to make more life-affirming choices and allow the spirit of God to flow more fully though us.

THE LAW OF OPPOSITES

When my feet fall heavy
and body wearies against the unforgiving ground,
I gentle lay my head to rest upon sweet thoughts
like feather down.

The more conscious of our true nature we are, the more choice we have. When we are confronting our internal enemies, those thoughts and feeling that are not compatible with our hopes and dreams of liberation, we have a choice in how we will face them and respond to them.

Sometimes the best action is to take no action, let them burn themselves out by remaining neutral. But, when we feel we must take a more dynamic approach, there is a simple technique we can use to neutralize the destructive thoughts without getting ensnared by them.

As discordant thoughts and feelings arise in our conscious minds, we take note of them; we don't push them away or push them down, we simply accept them as being there without labeling them as good or bad. The straightforward act of internalized acceptance has a neutralizing effect in the mind, but if we want to take a more assertive mental action, we can choose to insert into the mind the opposite thought or feeling.

Just as two objects cannot occupy the same space at the same time, neither can two thoughts occupy the same space in the mind at the same time. Thoughts can alternate from a negative pole to a positive pole, and back again, but they cannot rest at both poles simultaneously. This means we can introduce a positive, opposite thought or feeling to counteract the negative one we want to neutralize.

Thoughts and feeling are not static things. They ebb and flow; they continually change and evolve. After all, isn't it possible to originally dislike someone who eventually becomes a beloved close friend or companion? We can use this understanding to modify thoughts and feelings by presenting to the mind a contrary thought, idea, or feeling. For example, when we are nervous, we can choose to introduce calm into our psyche; we can create an internal dialogue that soothes feelings and levels out jagged thoughts. It is possible to change the vibration and effect of thoughts by choosing to think about and accept as a new concept, its opposite.

If we are feeling hate, we can choose to cultivate love and understanding. When we are restless, we can choose to be patient. We can replace judgmental thoughts with thoughts of compassion and caring. Knowing we are all humans struggling to thrive, our feelings of resentment can be replaced with acceptance and tolerance. For every negative feeling or emotion, its opposite can be intentionally used to counteract its influence over us.

The more aware we are of our thoughts and the effects they have on us, the greater the possibility to direct their movement and minimize their authority over us. We can become the architects of our thoughts and feelings, and reroute our own neural pathways for our benefit and spiritual evolution. In doing so, we prepare for our inevitable upliftment by the Consciousness-presence within us.

All human beings have a super power; we have the power of choice. We can choose how we think and feel. When we are awake and aware enough, we can choose to keep the thoughts that are most beneficial to us and discard those thoughts and feelings that keep us prisoners of our minds. There is freedom in truth, and the truth is we can choose how we think and feel and behave. We are not marionettes; we pull our own strings.

THE COMPANY WE KEEP

It is better to be alone than to be untrue

As our consciousness grows and our awareness expands, so too do our perceptions and perspectives. We no longer see the world through the eyes of unawake Souls. We have grown beyond our previously limited viewpoints, and the paradigms we were functioning in no longer work for us or hold any appeal.

The higher we climb the spiritual mountain, the thinner the air and the fewer the travelers. The truth is, there is a price to be paid for the unrelenting pursuit of the Divine. As we grow in spiritual and emotional maturity, we will have to leave our old world behind and venture into new and uncharted spiritual territory, and we often must do this on our own. No one can do for us, what we must do for ourselves, and this is never truer than when it comes to spiritual growth. We and we alone are responsible for our lives. We become more Self-reliant and Self- responsible as we expand our awareness into the profound depths of Spirit. People, friends, and even family members may fall away as our interests and interactions are integrated into and aligned with the priorities of spiritual evolution.

When we begin to think, speak, and act from higher and higher levels of consciousness, our vibrations become more refined and attuned to Spirit, and those vibrations radiating at lower frequencies may feel threatened or disconnected from us and we from them. Those of us who need to feel connected must often seek out new spiritual companions and communities whose beliefs and practices are more deeply allied with our own. But even in the company of more awake souls, we may still feel alone on our path. The cost of Spiritual awakening and liberation is a temporary sense of isolation and seclusion. If we accept this and move through it, the reward is a unity-of-being that was previously unimaginable.

It is when we permanently banish the false sense of a separate existence that all boundaries between the Soul and Spirit dissolve into the forgotten past. When we know God by experiencing our oneness with the omnipresent Spirit, aloneness and loneliness evaporate forever. It is then we realize the truth of our unified and integrated existence and we know we belong in this moment wherever and with whomever we find ourselves. The instant we realize we are an integrated part of the eternal unity of existence-being, all perception of distance and separation everlastingly fades away. We then become part of a universal spiritual family that will never abandon us, betray us, make us feel less, or leave us to our own devices. God, as all things and all creatures, is our forever home and we can rest and rely on its support and succor.

The most important company we can keep, is our own. The self-actualization/Self-realization process teaches us to rely solely on the indwelling spirit of God. To walk the spiritual path, we must learn to tread the cobblestones of intuition. When we rely on an external source of authority to make our decisions, we are not listening to the unerring word of God within us; it is possible to then miss the path God has already laid at our feet. When it comes to making decisions about our lives, the choice is ours and ours alone. We are responsible for the results of our decisions and we alone will experience the future those decisions create. Who better to rely on than the God indwelling? When we learn to rely on the definitive internal locus of authority, God; we are assured an outcome designed for our highest spiritual good.

We can listen, with respect, to the opinions of well-meaning people, but the final decision is to be made by only ourselves. If we do not listen to and act upon the internal authority that knows what is best for us, we risk getting lost in the labyrinth of social interaction. It is not an act of ego to make our decisions based on the still, quiet voice within, it is a spiritual imperative. That voice whispering through the silence sees our lives from an integrated universal perspective and equally takes into account not only what is best for our spiritual evolution, but what is best for everyone's spiritual evolution with whom we are interacting.

As we navigate life, it is likely we will move through and be a part of many groups and organizations. We will keep the company of people with varied backgrounds, perspectives, and opinions. But in the end, it is our own company we must learn to trust and rely on.

It is important to understand if we do find our spiritual tribe, we can interact and serve, but we need to make sure we do not become dependent on anyone or any group for our happiness. God and God alone should be our only anchor and our only dependency. The more we become reliant on the God indwelling, the more independent we will become. When we realize God is in us, we are whole and complete unto ourselves. It is then we see all people as our spiritual family and we can love them, but we are not attached to them and we are not dependent upon them.

Our best company is God, and God is found within us. The way we keep God's company is by keeping our attention turned inward. The silence within is the doorway to the kingdom of heaven; the key is our attention and focus. We are not islands in the ocean of consciousness; we are the ocean. Though we may be a wave of the ocean rising to crest this lifetime, one day we will recede back and rest only in the company of God.

THE ART OF INNER PEACE

I do not go to the woods to be alone;
I go because I'm lonely.

When we silence the mind and send it outward, there is only the vast and fruitless emptiness of the material realm. But when we silence the mind and send it inward; the fullness of spirit, unfettered by the senses, awaits our discovery. As our consciousness expands and our ego dissolves, there are moments when we break free from our restricted states of awareness. We rise above our attachments and aversions, likes and dislikes, expectations and disappointments, into an endless space filled with infinite potential. With this unshackling of the mind and detachment from the senses, comes the silence of existence-being and the Soul peace, born of Spirit, blossoms into the profoundness of realization. The deeper we dive into the Spirit within, the more subtle the experience, and the more profound the realization.

The often chaotic and sometimes frenzied, yet workaday world we live in, can pull us off-center as we struggle to move through it and overcome perceived obstacles and challenges. During these distractions, we must make an even greater effort to turn inward towards the source of our existence and anchor ourselves once again in the consciousness-presence of God within us.

The art of cultivating inner peace is mastered during the relentless pursuit of the divine presence of God. The consciousness-presence of God awaits our breakthrough and when the mind finally realizes what has been there all along, the soul heaves a great sigh of satisfaction and a lasting peace envelops us.

Sometimes, it is necessary to disconnect from the trappings of the modern world and stand clear of the technological mazes. We need moments when we can breathe unencumbered by the weight of the world and society; those moments when we can open our minds to the spiritual vastness within. We can generate those moments of inner discovery for ourselves by setting up a responsive and supportive outer environment.

A clean and well-organized room may be all we need to inspire spiritual greatness. At other times, we may require the healing that can only be found during an all-embracing immersion into nature.

When we walk deep the sylvan paths and commune thoughtful with God as mother, we open ourselves to its healing vibrations and the soothing balms of nature. Our minds slow, our breath falls in sync with the rhythm of our steps, and our very being resonates with the spirit of God expressing as the mountains and valleys, trees and streams, sand and seas. We can, if just for a short time, allow ourselves to be at peace. We can give ourselves permission to forget the worries of the world and connect with the spirit of God within. By doing this, we let go the troubles of the mind and awaken to clarity. With this clarity comes a promising spiritual vision of the mystical potentials awaiting us.

Nature itself does not bring us closer to God, our harmony with it stills all that we are not, and rouses the truth within us to declare its unmistakable presence. God, as mother, sings sweetly to us the lullaby of nature and we soften in her embrace; our defenses come down, our fears quiet, and we can breathe easy once more. The cacophony of thoughts pouring through the mind distill to a single thought of harmony and peace as we once again recognize our oneness with it through nature. The world, our world, becomes bright, clean and clear once again when we spend time communing with the mother of us all.

No matter where in the world or in life we find ourselves, we can always take a moment of internal seclusion to renew and reconnect with our truth. Even if it is just focusing on our breath in the midst of a crowded railway station or closing our eyes in quiet meditation on a plane, we can make the seemingly small effort to connect with the God awaiting us within. When we do this, we are consciously adjusting our awareness and allowing the wholeness of Spirit to blossom forward into our conscious minds. When Spirit rises to the fore of our thoughts, all that is not in harmony with it is stilled into silence. When silence reigns, peace flourishes. Eventually, with practice, we learn how-to-walk in peace by living in silence. The art of inner peace is found by surrendering to the silence, and silence is found within.

THE LAST THOUGHT

The Lord in heaven bends low
To better hear your prayer
And angels gently tremble
To see him frozen there

The greatest and most difficult spiritual lesson I have learned in this lifetime is to surrender and to accept. I realize I am not the doer; God is the only power, and God is the only manifestation of that power. The spirit of God within me is always moving in the direction of the source and fulfillment, and I can learn to accept it and participate with it, or resist it with an inflated sense of self-importance and false thoughts of being the creator myself.

We are not co-creators; we are conduits through which the spirit of the Creator flows. When we try to manipulate God and dictate how and when Spirit expresses, we are in a profound state of delusion. The moment we begin to think we are the doers, we have turned our backs on, and walked away from God. When we rationalize, because we are individual units of Spirit, we can take or make what we want from this world, we are unconsciously grasping at life and materialism. Grasping reveals the emptiness we feel is within us. When we realize the truth of our existence and all we need is waiting within, life will reflect only this completeness and all needs are then effortlessly met.

The only limitations grace has, are those we set upon it with feelings of unworthiness, doubt, fear, and guilt. These are the afflictions we know as our personal demons and our belief they have power over us keeps us from receiving the blessing that is the spirit of God expressing as us. But if we do the inner work of coming to terms with these demons and removing their power over us through acceptance and consciousness expansion, and if we integrate the process of self-actualization with the process of Self-realization, we set ourselves free and awaken to an Edenic consciousness awaiting within.

You and I have come to this world to overcome our doubts, fears, and misbeliefs. We have come to this world to banish the affliction of delusion. Being born into these bodies is a gift of grace affording us the opportunity to set ourselves free. If we squander the gift of life, the consequences are ours to experience.

There is no physical hell awaiting us because we reject religious canon. There is no judgment of God because we do not succeed in the eyes of others or fail to live up to the standards and mores of society. There is no penalty for leaving a church because we feel unfulfilled. The house of the Lord is within us and around us, and the doorway is the silence found in introspection and meditation. We, and only we, can light the candle of Spirit in dwelling. No church or religious organization can do that for us, just as no church or religious organization can save us.

Salvation is awakening to the innermost tabernacle of God inside us. It is not the false belief that an intermediary can forgive our sins as a stand-in for God. If we are to rise up and take back our own sanctity, we must discard the false indoctrinations of religious evangelistic clerics blindly leading us down the path of confusion with their misinterpretations and their misunderstandings of the profundities of scripture.

Hell is the unawareness that God is in us and it is experienced when we accept that there is any power or expression other than God. When we learn to rely on God and only God, salvation and redemption are assured. At the moment of absolute acceptance that there is only the one consciousness-presence expressing as us and the world, the delusion that has kept us imprisoned dissolves into the abyss of unknowing.

We are here to awaken to the truth, and the truth is, there isn't only one God; there is only God. Any sense of separation, ego, is a lie. We are one with the Creator of this manifest entirety. We only have to rouse from our slumber of delusion to the reality of our existence. The less we resist the awakening process and the more we participate with it, the sooner we take up our reason for being here and the sooner we are forever free. The beauty and majesty of spiritual paradise awaits our discovery and it is secreted beneath the layers of our self-doubt and false sense of unworthiness. The kingdom of God is awaiting our discovery within us. We need only rise up and accept it. The Journey to Remembrance is a journey of Self-discovery and Self-realization.

I DREAMT A MOST BEAUTIFUL DREAM
I must share the holiness of

I dreamt of the rain coming down
And we stepped out onto the open plains
To feel it wash over our faces and bodies
And we could sing in my dream and sing we did

We began to sing and dance and praise
God for this perfect day of rain he made
Our feet stamped out a slide and pound rhythm
I looked down to see the dust on my feet become ochre mud
And we could sing in my dream and sing we did

With one voice lifted high and strong and sent far
We sang Hosanna in the rain as we pound our feet to the ground
We sang Hosanna in the rain in clear voices carried to heaven
We sang Hosanna in the rain as one with the Lord
And we could sing in my dream and sing we did unafraid

Then I awoke from my dream of rain and singing and stamping
Wrapped sacred in a stillness and a silence
The rain wet on my face as I cried at the loss
Of joy and harmony and the loss of the rain on my face
But we can sing of God in our dreams and sing we will

Made in the USA
Middletown, DE
05 February 2024

48632673R00051